THIS BOOK BELONGS TO

_____

_____

The New Testament

GALILEE, WHERE JESUS GREW UP, is-a hilly area at the heart of which is the Sea of Galilee, a huge freshwater lake. In Jesus' time there were a number of thriving communities, such as Capernaum, Bethsaida, and Tiberias, around the shores of the lake. There were also several important trade routes through the area. This brought the Galileans into contact with people from many countries.

Together with other Jewish people from Galilee, Jesus and his family traveled to Jerusalem in Judea for major festivals such as Passover. The long journey, on foot or donkey, would have taken them south along the fertile Jordan valley, avoiding Samaria, to the low-lying area at the north end of the Dead Sea.

Jerusalem, in the region of Judea, was the most important Jewish religious center. It was very crowded during Jewish festivals, but it was always busy with merchants traveling there from different parts of the Roman empire.

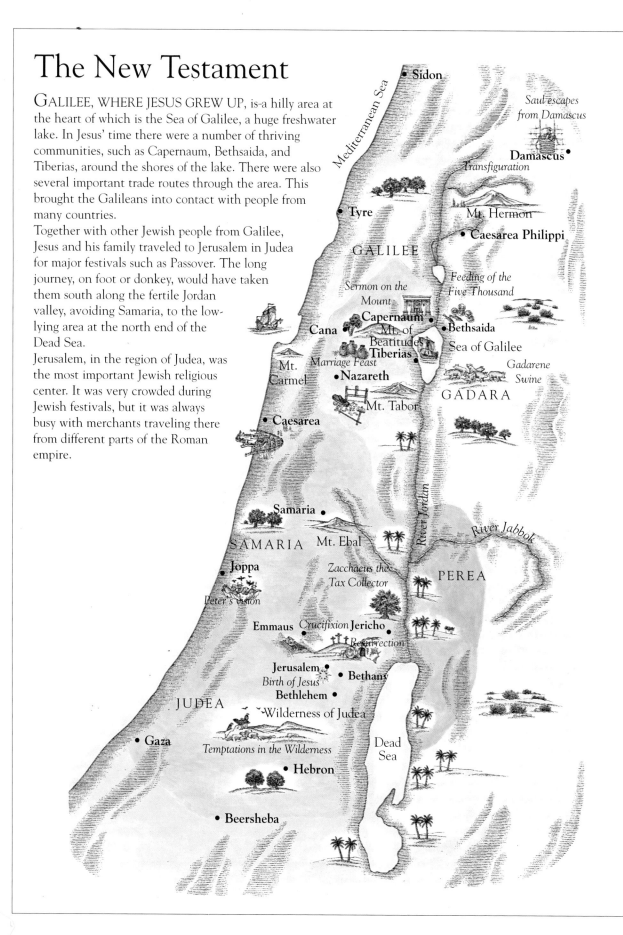

The Birth of Jesus

• And other Bible stories •

Retold *by* Selina Hastings

A DK PUBLISHING BOOK

Art Editor Shirley Gwillym
Project Editor Marie Greenwood
Senior Editor Emma Johnson
Designer Sarah Cowley
Additional design by
Heather Blackham, Muffy Dodson
Production Ruth Cobb, Marguerite Fenn
Managing Editor Susan Peach
Managing Art Editor Jacquie Gulliver

Introduction and section openers written by
Geoffrey Marshall-Taylor

CONSULTANTS
Educational Consultant
Geoffrey Marshall-Taylor,
Executive Producer, BBC Education,
Responsible for religious radio programmes
for schools

Historical Consultant
Carole Mendleson
Western Asiatic Department
British Museum, London

Religious Consultants
Reverend Stephen Motyer
London Bible College

Bernadette Chapman and
Father Philip Walshe
St Mary's College, Twickenham

Published in the United States by
DK PUBLISHING, Inc.,
95 Madison Avenue, New York, NY 10016

The Children's Illustrated Bible
Copyright © 1994 Dorling Kindersley Limited, London
Text copyright © 1994 Selina Hastings
The right of Selina Hastings to be identified as the Author
of this Work has been asserted by her in accordance with
the Copyright Designs and Patents Act 1988.

A CIP catalog record for this book is available from the
Library of Congress.

ISBN 07513-5482-1
Reproduced by Colourscan, Singapore
Printed and bound in Spain by Artes Graficas
Toledo S.A. D.L.TO: 1193-1966

Extracts from the Authorised Version of the Bible (The
King James Bible), the rights of which are vested in the
Crown, are reproduced by permission of the Crown's
Patentee, Cambridge University Press.

CONTENTS

Introduction to the New Testament

THE NEW TESTAMENT is made up of 27 books. The first four, the gospels of Matthew, Mark, Luke, and John describe the life, death, and resurrection of Jesus. The Acts of the Apostles tells of the growth of the Christian church and the journeys of St. Paul. The Epistles are letters from Christian leaders to Christians in the newly spreading churches. The book of Revelation contains letters to seven churches and writings about the future reign of Jesus in the world.

The Gospels

"Gospel" means "good news." The words of the gospels were first passed by word of mouth from person to person. Many people believe that Mark's gospel was the first to be written down and that Matthew and Luke referred to Mark's book in their own writings. John's gospel is quite different. It does not describe as many events in Jesus' life or include any of his parables. It concentrates on explaining who Jesus was and what he taught.

The gospels do not tell us everything about the life of Jesus. They concentrate on the three years before his death and on selected events and incidents during this time. They were written by his close followers to show to others why they believed that Jesus was the Messiah, the Son of God. Their purpose was to get across the message of Jesus' teaching to people living at the time, and to leave a written account for future generations.

THE LINDISFARNE GOSPELS
The Gospel writers were sometimes represented by living creatures: Matthew by an angel, Mark by a lion, Luke by an ox, and John by an eagle, shown here in these manuscript illustrations from the 7th-century Lindisfarne Gospels.

Early Editions of the Bible

The New Testament books were first written down on papyrus scrolls, an early form of paper made from reeds. Christians then began to copy them onto sheets of papyrus, which were bound and placed between two pieces of wood or tablets. This form of early book was called a codex.

Papyrus plant

The oldest part of the New Testament is from St. John's Gospel and dates from about AD 125. A complete New Testament in codex form was found at St. Catherine's monastery at the foot of Mount Sinai in 1844. The Codex Sinaiticus is in

St. Matthew

St. Mark

St. Luke

St. John

Codex Sinaiticus

ST. CATHERINE'S MONASTERY, MOUNT SINAI
The Codex Sinaiticus was found at St. Catherine's
monastery, shown above in a painting by David Roberts.

Greek and dates from the 4th century AD.
Manuscript fragments of the New Testament can
be traced to the 2nd century.

As the Christian church spread, the New
Testament was translated into Latin and other
languages. It was not until 1382 that the first
complete version of the Bible in English was
published. It was translated by John Wycliffe and,
at that time, the words were still copied by hand.

The first printed Bible was the Gutenberg,
which appeared in 1456 with text in Latin.
Printed translations in other languages soon
followed, but it was not until 1535 that the first
complete English Bible was published by Miles
Coverdale. The first Authorized Version of the
Bible appeared in 1611 in the form of the King
James Bible. This was one of the great

achievements of King James I of England's reign.
There are now many versions of the Bible. It has
been translated into over 1,900 languages. This
means that most people in the world can hear it
being read or can read it for themselves in words
they can understand. This is important to Christians
who believe that the Bible is one of the main ways
in which people can find out about God's love for
the world.

*The New Testament
tells of Jesus'
teachings and how
people of all ages
were drawn to him.*

A Son for Zechariah

ALTAR OF INCENSE
As a priest, Zechariah would probably have burnt the incense on a four-horned altar, such as the one above. These altars were also thought of as safe places. If a person grasped one of the horns, then the holiness of the altar protected them from harm. It was a great honor for Zechariah when he was chosen to offer incense. It would have been the only time he was allowed to enter the temple sanctuary, or holy place.

"FEAR NOT, ZECHARIAH: FOR THY PRAYER IS HEARD; AND THY WIFE ELIZABETH SHALL BEAR THEE A SON, AND THOU SHALT CALL HIS NAME JOHN. AND THOU SHALT HAVE JOY AND GLADNESS; AND MANY SHALL REJOICE AT HIS BIRTH."
LUKE 1:13-14

An angel appears before Zechariah and tells him he will have a son

Zechariah does not believe the angel, and is struck dumb

IN THE DAYS OF KING HEROD, there lived in Judea a priest named Zechariah. He and his wife Elizabeth were good people, who had always obeyed the word of God. Their one sorrow was that they were childless. Now they were growing old, and had given up all hope of ever having a family.

There came a time when Zechariah, serving at the temple in Jerusalem, was chosen by lot to burn incense in the sanctuary. This was at an hour when the people were praying in an outer courtyard.

As Zechariah stood watching the fragrant smoke rise from the altar, he saw an angel standing before him. Frightened, he stumbled back, but the angel spoke to him gently.

"I am Gabriel," he said. "I have come from the Lord to bring you good news. Your prayers shall be answered, and your wife will give birth to a son, whose name shall be John. He will be a great joy to you both, and will bring much happiness and peace to the world. He will be great in the eyes of the Lord, and through him many people will turn to God."

"But how can this happen?" Zechariah exclaimed in disbelief. "After all, I am an old man, and my wife Elizabeth is past the age to bear children."

"I am an angel of the Lord," said Gabriel sternly. "I have been sent by God to speak to you and tell you this good news. Because you have doubted my word, which will be fulfilled in its own time, you will be unable to speak until what I have told you comes true."

Meanwhile, the crowd outside began to grow restless, wondering why the priest was so long in the temple before coming out to them. When Zechariah finally appeared, he could not say a word: all he could do was make gestures, and the people quickly realized that he must have seen a vision.

Having completed his duties, Zechariah returned home to his wife, and as the angel predicted, Elizabeth soon became pregnant. She stayed quietly at home, rejoicing that God had chosen her to bear this child.

INCENSE SHOVEL
Zechariah may have used an incense shovel, such as the one above, to carry burning coals to the altar. Incense was sprinkled on the coals to produce a fragrant smoke. The rising smoke symbolized the prayers of the people going up to God.

Unable to speak, Zechariah makes gestures to the people

An Angel Appears to Mary

I N THE TOWN OF NAZARETH in Galilee, the angel Gabriel appeared to a young woman called Mary. Mary was promised in marriage to Joseph, who was descended from the family of David.

"The Lord is with you!" said Gabriel. "You are the most fortunate of women!"

Mary was troubled by the angel's greeting, and wondered why he had come to see her. "Do not be afraid," Gabriel reassured her. "God has chosen you to be the mother of a child, a son, who shall be called

NAZARETH
Mary and Joseph lived in Nazareth, in the northern province of Galilee. This little town lay in a sheltered valley set in hills about 5 miles (8 km) from the important trading town of Sepphoris. Above is Nazareth today, with the Church of the Annunciation in the center of the picture. The Annunciation – the announcing – refers to the angel Gabriel's words to Mary, when he tells her that she will be the mother of Jesus.

AND THE ANGEL SAID UNTO HER, "FEAR NOT, MARY: FOR THOU HAST FOUND FAVOR WITH GOD. AND, BEHOLD, THOU SHALT CONCEIVE IN THY WOMB, AND BRING FORTH A SON, AND SHALT CALL HIS NAME JESUS."
LUKE 1:30-31

Mary is troubled by the angel's greeting, and wonders why he has come to see her

Jesus. He will be great and his kingdom will never end."

"But how is this possible?" Mary asked. "I am still a girl, and not yet married."

"The Holy Spirit will come to you, and God's grace will be with you, for your child will be known as the Son of God."

At these words, Mary knelt before Gabriel, and with head bowed, replied, "I am obedient to God's will, and shall be prepared for whatever you wish me to do."

She looked up, but the angel had gone.

The angel Gabriel tells Mary that she will give birth to a son, who will be called Jesus

ANGEL GABRIEL
This page from an illuminated manuscript shows the angel Gabriel appearing to Mary. Gabriel was an archangel, or angel of high rank. He brought messages to God's people about the coming of the Messiah, the saviour promised by God. Gabriel is one of three angels, the others being Michael and Raphael, who are mentioned by name in the Bible.

The Birth of John

Mary visits Elizabeth at her home in Judea

FLAT-ROOFED HOUSES
The houses in Judea and the surrounding area were built of mud bricks, or rough stones as in the picture above. People found the flat roofs of the houses useful. They could dry fruit and grain on them, as well as dry their clothes. In hot weather they might even sleep out on the roof.

MARY HURRIED INTO the hills of Judea to visit her cousin Elizabeth. As Mary entered the house and called out in greeting, Elizabeth felt the baby leap for joy in her womb. She felt the presence of God all around her, making her aware that the woman standing in front of her was the mother of the son of God.

"You are the most blessed of all women!" Elizabeth exclaimed. "When I heard your voice, I felt my baby move inside me. How honored I am that you have come here to be with me!"

Then Mary sang a song of praise:

"My soul sings of the glory of the Lord,
And my spirit rejoices in God who is my saviour.
He has looked with kindness on me, his devoted servant,
And because he has honored me, future generations will
bless my name.
He is always merciful to those who love and obey him,
But he humbles the proud and the hard-hearted.
Always he feeds the hungry, but to the rich and greedy
he gives nothing.
The Lord is great and holy is his name."

Mary stayed with Elizabeth for three months, then returned home to Nazareth.

Soon afterward, Elizabeth gave birth to a son. There was great rejoicing by all her family and neighbors that God should have shown her such favor. On the eighth day, the time came for the baby to be circumcised.

"He must be called Zechariah, after his father," said her relations.

"No," said Elizabeth. "His name is John."

"But no one in your family is called John," they said, and they turned to Zechariah to ask what he wanted to call the child.

Zechariah, who still could not speak, signaled for writing materials. Then to the surprise of those around him, he wrote in large letters, HIS NAME IS JOHN. At that same moment he found he could talk, and at once started to thank God and to sing hymns of praise.

Soon the story had spread throughout the Judean hills that a holy child had been born to Elizabeth. All who heard knew that this was a great event, and that the Lord was with the child John.

EN KEREM
The pretty little town of En Kerem, whose name means "vineyard spring," is set in the Judean hills. It is traditionally believed to be the hometown of Zechariah and Elizabeth, and the birthplace of John the Baptist.

Zechariah

Elizabeth

Zechariah writes a message that they must call his son John

WRITING TOOLS
Zechariah may have written his message on paper made from the dried stems of the papyrus plant. He would have used a reed pen dipped in black ink to write with.

The Birth of Jesus

An angel appears to Joseph in a dream and tells him not to be afraid to make Mary his wife

Mary is soon to give birth

saw

plane

mallet

ax

CARPENTER'S TOOLS
As a carpenter, Joseph would have used tools, such as the ones above, to make furniture, doors, farm tools, carts, and to repair houses. Joseph would have passed on the skills of his trade to Jesus.

JOSEPH WAS an honorable man, and when he saw that Mary was expecting a child, his first thought was to protect her from scandal and to quietly release her from her betrothal. But an angel came to him and said, "Do not be afraid to take Mary for your wife. She has conceived this child by the Holy Spirit. She will give birth to a son, whose name shall be Jesus."

Soon after Joseph and Mary were married, the Emperor Augustus passed a law that everyone should return to their hometown so that a count could be made of every person in the empire. Joseph went with

Joseph travels with Mary to Bethlehem in Judea

RIDING ON A DONKEY
Traditionally, Mary is thought to have ridden on a donkey from Nazareth to Bethlehem – a distance of about 70 miles (110 km). Donkeys were the most common form of transportation in Jesus' time, and were used by both rich and poor people.

SHE WRAPPED HIM IN SWADDLING CLOTHES, AND LAID HIM IN A MANGER; BECAUSE THERE WAS NO ROOM FOR THEM IN THE INN.
LUKE 2:7

Mary lays the baby Jesus in a manger

Mary, who was soon to give birth, to Bethlehem in Judea.

When at last they arrived, they found the city full of people. The streets were crowded, and every house and lodging already full. Joseph, anxious because he knew that the time of the baby's birth was near, searched and searched, but could find nowhere to stay. Eventually, worn out by their journey, they took shelter in a stable, and there during the night Mary's son was born. She wrapped him in strips of linen, as was the custom, and gently laid him in a manger, where the animals fed. There was nowhere else for the baby to sleep.

The Shepherds' Visit

IN THE FIELDS NEAR BETHLEHEM there were shepherds, tending their flocks. Suddenly a brilliant light blazed through the darkness, and an angel appeared. The shepherds, terrified, hid their eyes, but the angel reassured them. "I bring you good news, today in Bethlehem a child has been born, who will be the saviour of all people. You will find him in a manger." Then the night sky was filled with heavenly beings, and the angels sang in praise of God. They spoke of peace on earth and friendship between everyone.

"We must go at once to see the child," the shepherds said. They hurried to the town where they soon found Mary, Joseph, and the baby in the stable. Excitedly, they described what they had seen and heard, and went away praising God. Only Mary was silent, thinking quietly to herself of all that had happened.

SHEPHERD'S TOOLS
Shepherds would often have to stay out all night, keeping watch over their flocks. They kept warm by wearing camel-hair cloaks, or cloaks made from sheepskin, like this present-day shepherd's coat. A shepherd could use the hook on the end of his crook to pull or lift a sheep out of danger. His wooden rod had pieces of flint or nails driven into the end. He used this to drive away wild animals. He could use the wooden feeding bowl to bring water to an injured sheep.

THE ANGEL OF THE LORD
CAME UPON THEM, AND THE
GLORY OF THE LORD SHONE
ROUND ABOUT THEM: AND
THEY WERE SORE AFRAID
LUKE 2:9

*Angels appear to the shepherds and
bring news of Jesus' birth*

AND THEY CAME WITH HASTE,
AND FOUND MARY AND
JOSEPH, AND THE BABE LYING
IN A MANGER.
LUKE 2:16

*The shepherds hurry to
Bethlehem, where they find Mary
and Joseph with the baby Jesus*

The Presentation in the Temple

"LORD, NOW LETTEST THOU THY SERVANT DEPART IN PEACE, ACCORDING TO THY WORD: FOR MINE EYES HAVE SEEN THY SALVATION."
LUKE 2:29-30

Simeon

Joseph

Mary

Mary and Joseph watch as Simeon takes the baby Jesus in his arms

EIGHT DAYS AFTER HE WAS BORN, the baby was circumcised and given the name Jesus, as the angel had instructed. Mary and Joseph then took him to Jerusalem to present him to the Lord, and to make an offering, which according to custom could be either a pair of doves or two young pigeons.

In Jerusalem there lived a man called Simeon, a good man who had led a holy life. God had said to him that he would not die before he had set eyes on the Messiah. When Mary, carrying her child, and Joseph entered the temple, Simeon was already there. He had been guided by the Holy Spirit, and knew at once that he was in the presence of the saviour promised by God.

Taking Jesus gently in his arms, he gave grateful thanks to the Lord. "O Lord, now I may die in peace, for you have granted me what my heart most desired. Now I have seen with my own eyes the child who is to be a glory to all people!"

As he spoke, a very old woman came shuffling out from the shadows. Her name was Anna, and she had lived nearly all her life in the temple, spending every day and most of the night in fasting and prayers. She, too, thanked God that she had been allowed to see the child, and told all who could hear that Jesus would be the saviour of Jerusalem.

Mary and Joseph stood amazed as they listened to what was said about the child. Then, when all had been done, they left Jerusalem and returned home.

OLD AGE
Anna was an old prophetess who prayed and fasted in the temple day and night. Her holiness was rewarded when she saw Jesus in the temple. In the Bible, age is a sign of wisdom and goodness. To reach old age is seen as a blessing from God.

Anna comes forward to see Jesus

The Wise Men

*Wise men arrive from the east and are
sent for by King Herod*

NOW WHEN JESUS WAS BORN
IN BETHLEHEM OF JUDEA IN
THE DAYS OF HEROD THE KING,
BEHOLD, THERE CAME WISE
MEN FROM THE EAST TO
JERUSALEM, SAYING, "WHERE
IS HE THAT IS BORN KING OF
THE JEWS? FOR WE HAVE SEEN
HIS STAR IN THE EAST, AND
ARE COME TO WORSHIP HIM."
MATTHEW 2:1-2

*Herod questions the wise men closely about the
star they have seen over Bethlehem*

FROM THE EAST
It is not known where the
wise men, or magi, came
from. One idea is that
they journeyed from
Persia, Babylonia, and
Arabia. They may have
been astrologers, who
read the stars for signs
and omens. The wise men
represented the Gentiles,
or nonJewish people, who
would worship Jesus.

NEWS OF THE BIRTH of Jesus spread far and wide. A
group of wise men traveled from the east to
Jerusalem. When they arrived, they asked
everyone, "Where is the child? Where is the one who has
been born king of the Jews? We have seen his star and have
come to worship him."

Now Herod was king of Judea, and stories soon reached his ears of
the coming of the messiah, a child born to rule. Deeply troubled and
determined to put to death any rival, he summoned together all the
priests and lawyers of the Jewish people, and asked them in what city
the child was to be born.

"In Bethlehem," they told him.

Then privately, Herod sent for the wise men, and pretending to be
as religious as they, questioned them closely about the star: where

they had seen it, what time it had appeared. "Go to Bethlehem," he said. "Make a thorough search for the child, and when you have found him, come and tell me, for I, too, wish to go and worship him."

So the wise men left Jerusalem and took the road for Bethlehem. The star guided them all the way, until, as they drew near the walls of the little town, it shone even brighter and stopped quite still over the place where Jesus was.

As they entered the house, they saw Mary and her small child, and falling to their knees, they worshiped him. Then they opened the heavy boxes they had carried with them, and spread out on the floor the magnificent gifts they had brought. They gave the baby Jesus gifts of gold, frankincense, and myrrh. Then, having been warned in a dream not to return to Herod, they went back to their own countries by another route.

THREE WISE MEN?
This mosaic showing the wise men is in Ravenna, Italy. The Bible does not say how many wise men there were, but the common belief is that there were three, because of the three gifts they carried with them.

The wise men bring gifts of gold, frankincense, and myrrh

They enter the house and see Mary and her child, Jesus

THREE GIFTS
The wise men brought gifts of gold, frankincense, and myrrh. Frankincense was a perfumed resin, burned in honor of God. Myrrh was a scented gum used to prepare the body for burial. The gifts had symbolic meanings. Gold honored Jesus as a king, frankincense honored Jesus as God, and myrrh was a sign that Jesus was a man and would die.

The Flight into Egypt

Joseph, Mary, and the child Jesus leave Bethlehem during the night and head for Egypt

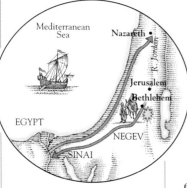

JOURNEY TO SAFETY
Mary and Joseph faced a difficult journey across 75 miles (121 km) of desert land before they reached Egypt, a country often used as a place of refuge. After Herod's death, the family went to Nazareth in Galilee.

SOON AFTER the wise men had left, an angel appeared to Joseph in a dream. "Take Mary and the child and go at once to Egypt. There is no time to lose. Herod's men are searching for the child, and if they find him, they will kill him."

At this Joseph awoke, and told Mary what they must do. Quietly they crept out of the house, and in the darkness made their way through the narrow streets of the town and out into open country. The journey took many days, but at last they arrived safely in Egypt; and there they stayed.

Herod, meanwhile, realized that the wise men had tricked him and would not be returning to tell him where Jesus was. He fell into a passionate rage, and screamed at anyone who dared come near, threatening with fearful punishment those who stood in his way. Summoning the officer of his guard, he gave an order that every male child in and near Bethlehem under the age of two years should be put to death. And this was done.

Soon after Herod himself died. Again the angel came to Joseph while he slept. "Your enemies are no more," he said. "It is now safe for you to return to your homeland." So the family left Egypt. But when Joseph learned that Herod had been succeeded by his son, Archelaus, as ruler of Judea, he was afraid. So they traveled farther north, and settled in the city of Nazareth in Galilee.

On Herod's orders, every
male child in Bethlehem
under the age of two
years is put to death

Jesus Is Found in the Temple

VERY YEAR AT THE FESTIVAL OF PASSOVER, Joseph and Mary went to Jerusalem, as was the custom. When Jesus was twelve, they took him with them. After the celebrations had finished, they set off for home, making the long journey, as they always did, with a party of friends and relatives. They had been on the road for a whole day before they realized that Jesus was not with them. At first they thought he must be with some of their friends' children; but he was nowhere to be seen.

Anxiously Mary and Joseph returned to Jerusalem, and for three days they searched the city without success. Desperate with worry they decided to go to the temple. And there they saw Jesus. He was sitting in the middle of a group of wise men and teachers, talking,

BAR MITZVAH
Jesus went to Jerusalem when he was 12, a time when he was preparing to become a Jewish adult. Today, a Jewish boy will celebrate his *bar mitzvah*, when, at the age of 13, he enters Jewish life as an adult.

Jesus sits in the middle of a group of wise men, talking

listening, and answering questions. All these
distinguished men were amazed at the wisdom and
understanding of this child of twelve.

"How could you have left us like that?" his parents
asked him. "Why did you not tell us where you were
going to be? For three days we have been searching
everywhere for you."

"But why did you need to search?" said Jesus, puzzled.
"Did you not know that I would be in my father's house?"

Mary and Joseph did not understand what he meant by this.
Then Jesus left the temple, and returned with his parents to
Nazareth and was obedient to them.

HEROD'S TEMPLE
Herod's temple was the
center of Jewish religious
life. It was built by Herod
the Great on the site of
Solomon's temple.
Herod, wishing to win
favor with the Jewish
people, had wanted the
temple to be as splendid
as Solomon's. Work
began in 20 BC. The
temple opened in 9 BC,
but was not completely
finished until AD 64. Six
years later it was
destroyed by the Romans.
The temple was built of
cream-colored stone, and
had marble columns. It
shone so brightly in the
sun that people found it
difficult to look at it
directly (see page 17).

*Mary and Joseph, who have
been searching for Jesus, find
him in the temple*

*The wise men and teachers are
amazed at the wisdom and
understanding of Jesus*

AFTER THREE DAYS THEY
FOUND HIM IN THE TEMPLE,
SITTING IN THE MIDST OF THE
DOCTORS, BOTH HEARING
THEM, AND ASKING THEM
QUESTIONS.
LUKE 2:46

John Baptizes Jesus

John preaches to the people to repent

People flock to hear him

DESERT FOOD
John the Baptist ate locusts and wild honey in the desert. The honey would have been made by wild bees. They were common in Palestine, and nested in holes in rocks and trees. Locusts contain fat and protein, and are often eaten in areas where meat is scarce. They can be fried, boiled, dried, or eaten raw. Honey may be added to take away the bitterness.

DEEP IN THE WILDERNESS OF JUDEA, John the Baptist wandered from place to place, preaching. He wore only a rough coat made of camel's hair and a leather belt, and he lived on locusts and wild honey. "Repent! Repent!" he urged all who would listen. "Turn away from wickedness. The day of God's kingdom will soon be here!"

People flocked to hear him, pouring out in great crowds from Jerusalem and the Jordan Valley and all the towns of Judea. "What must we do?" they asked.

"Give as much as you can to others, do not hurt anyone, and never be false," he told them.

Group after group came to confess their sins, after which John baptized them in the River Jordan. "I baptize you with water," he told them. "But one will come after me who will baptize you with the fire of the Holy Spirit! He is a man so good and pure that I am unworthy even to unfasten his sandals."

"Are you Christ?" they asked him.

"No, I am the forerunner of Christ, the voice of one crying in the wilderness."

Jesus came from Galilee to hear the preacher, and to be baptized in

The people come to John to be baptized in the River Jordan

John baptizes Jesus

BAPTISM

Ritual cleansing was important to Jewish people. When John baptized people by lowering them into the water, he was obeying Jewish law, but giving it a new meaning. The purpose of John's baptisms was to rid people of wrongdoing, in expectation of Jesus' coming. Today, baptism is practiced by many Christians throughout the world upon entering into the Christian faith.

DOVE

At Jesus' baptism, the Holy Spirit took the form of a dove, and this bird has remained a symbol of the Holy Spirit. The dove also symbolizes peace, love, gentleness, and forgiveness.

the Jordan. But John said, "It is not right that I should do this. It is you who should baptize me."

"Let us do what God asks of us," Jesus replied, and he walked down to the banks of the river and into the water. As soon as John had baptized Jesus, the sky opened, and the Holy Spirit appeared in the form of a dove, and the voice of God was heard, saying, "This is my beloved son, in whom I am well pleased."

The Temptations in the Wilderness

DEVIL
The devil has often been portrayed as a winged creature with horns, as in this ceiling painting. In the Bible, the devil, or Satan, opposes God in every way.

J ESUS WENT INTO THE WILDERNESS for forty days to fast and pray, alone except for the wild beasts and birds of the desert. At the end of this time, he was exhausted and faint from hunger. Then the devil came to tempt him. "If, as you claim, you really are the son of God," said Satan, "then turn these stones into bread!"

"The scriptures say that man cannot live on bread alone, but must find strength from God's words," said Jesus.

Satan made a second attempt. Taking them to Jerusalem, he led

Jesus is alone, except for the wild beasts and birds of the desert

The devil tempts Jesus to turn stones into bread

Jesus up to the highest point on the temple roof. "Throw yourself down from here," he said. "The son of God, so we are told, is surrounded by angels, and cannot come to harm."

"Scripture says you shall not put God to the test," said Jesus.

Then the devil took Jesus to the top of a high mountain, and from there showed him all the kingdoms of the world. "I will make you lord of these lands," said the tempter, "if you will only kneel down and worship me!"

"Get behind me, Satan!" Jesus shouted. "It is God alone whom you should worship!"

At these words, the devil disappeared, knowing he was defeated. Angels then appeared from out of the sky to tend to Jesus.

JUDEAN WILDERNESS
The wilderness of Judea is a wild and lonely area west of the Jordan Valley. Alone in the desert, Jesus showed great strength in the face of temptation.

The devil tempts Jesus to throw himself down from the temple roof

On the top of a mountain the devil tempts Jesus with the kingdoms of the world

JESUS ANSWERED HIM, SAYING, "IT IS WRITTEN, THAT MAN SHALL NOT LIVE BY BREAD ALONE, BUT BY EVERY WORD OF GOD."
LUKE 4:4

Jesus Calls His Disciples

Jesus tells Peter and Andrew to cast their nets into the water, and the nets fill with fish

FISHING
Fishing was an important industry around the Sea of Galilee. Lines and hooks were sometimes used, as above, but nets were more common. At least four of Jesus' 12 disciples were fishermen.

ESUS WAS LIVING and teaching in Capernaum, a town by the Sea of Galilee. One day, as he was walking by the shore, he saw two fishing boats drawn up on land, their owners nearby, cleaning and mending their nets. Jesus stepped onto the nearest boat, and began talking to the crowds that soon gathered. After a while he said to the boat's owner, Simon Peter, "Let us go out a little way onto the lake."

When they were a short distance from land, Jesus told Simon Peter and his brother, Andrew, to throw their nets into the water. "But there are no fish," they said. "We have fished all night, and caught nothing."

However, they did as Jesus told them, and to their astonishment their nets filled instantly with such a weight of fish that they were unable to pull them up. They signaled to their partners in the other boat to help them, and together they hauled the nearly breaking nets on board.

When the two brothers saw the miraculous catch, they and their friends, James and John, the sons of Zebedee, fell down on their knees, terrified. But Jesus said, "Do not be afraid. Come, follow me, and I will make you fishers of men and women." So having brought their boats back to shore, they left their nets and the tools of their trade and followed Jesus.

Jesus traveled with his disciples throughout Galilee, preaching in the synagogues, spreading the word of God, and treating the sick. Men and women with every kind of illness and disease – some paralyzed, some epileptic, others racked with pain or tormented by horrific dreams – all came to be healed. People came from far and wide to hear him speak, not only from Galilee itself, but from Jerusalem, Judea, and from way beyond Jordan.

One day Jesus passed a man called Matthew, a collector of taxes.

He worked for the ruling Romans and so was distrusted by the people. Jesus said to him, too, "Come, follow me." And Matthew, without a word, left his post and followed him.

When Jesus returned to his house and sat down to dinner with his companions, a throng of people came to join him, many of them well-known as sinners. The Pharisees, shocked to see this good man in such bad company, questioned some of his friends. "Why does your master mix with rascals like these?" But Jesus heard their sneering words, and replied, "It is not the healthy who need a doctor, but the sick: I have not come to ask good men to change their ways, but the sinners, for it is they who need me."

Jesus went alone to the top of a high mountain, where he stayed all night in prayer. The next day he called his followers together, and chose twelve of them to be his disciples. To each one he gave special powers of preaching and healing. The twelve were: Simon Peter and his brother, Andrew; James and John, the sons of Zebedee; Philip, Bartholomew, Thomas, Matthew the tax collector, James, Thaddaeus, Simon the Zealot, and Judas Iscariot.

Jesus asks Matthew, a collector of taxes, to come and follow him

AND HE SAITH UNTO THEM, "FOLLOW ME, AND I WILL MAKE YOU FISHERS OF MEN." **MATTHEW 4:19**

Jesus chooses twelve disciples, to whom he gives special powers of preaching and healing

Matthew

Simon

Philip

Jesus

James, brother of John

John

Andrew

Simon Peter

Thomas

Bartholomew

James

Thaddaeus

Judas

The Sermon on the Mount

*Jesus preaches on
the mountainside*

Jesus

*The crowds gather and listen
to Jesus' words*

BLESSED ARE THE POOR IN
SPIRIT: FOR THEIRS IS THE
KINGDOM OF HEAVEN.
BLESSED ARE THEY THAT
MOURN: FOR THEY SHALL BE
COMFORTED. BLESSED ARE
THE MEEK: FOR THEY SHALL
INHERIT THE EARTH.
MATTHEW 5:4-5

THE CROWDS WHO CAME to hear Jesus were very great. So that everyone could see and hear him, he went a little way up the mountainside. This is what he said:

Blessed are the gentle, for they shall inherit the earth. Blessed are the merciful, for they shall be shown mercy. Blessed are the pure in heart, for they shall see God. Blessed are the peacemakers, for they shall be called the children of God. Blessed are those who are humble, those who are just, those who try to do right, those who suffer persecution – all of them will be rewarded in the kingdom of Heaven.

Do not keep your good qualities hidden, but let them shine out like a candle lighting up a dark house. When a lamp is lit, it is not put under a bowl, but placed where it can brighten the whole room.

I am not here to destroy the law, or contradict the words of the prophets. I am here to uphold them, for it is essential that the law be obeyed.

You have heard it said, you shall not kill. But those who keep murderous thoughts in their minds are also to blame. You must be able to forgive whoever has made you angry.

The old law speaks of an eye for an eye, and a tooth for a tooth, but if someone strikes you on the right cheek, it is better to turn the left cheek so that he may strike that, too.

It is easy to love your friends, but it is as important to love your enemies also, and be kind to those who turn against you.

You should never boast of your good deeds, but do them secretly.

You cannot value both God and money.

When you pray, do not do so in the open where everyone can see, but alone in your room. Talk directly to God, and say what is in your heart. Pray using these words: "Our Lord who is in Heaven, holy is your name. Your kingdom is coming. We will obey you on Earth as you are obeyed in Heaven. Give us our daily food. Forgive us our sins, as we forgive the sins of others. Do not lead us into temptation, but save us from evil."

Do not worry about what you wear or what you eat and drink. The birds in the air do not sow wheat or store it in barns, and yet the heavenly Lord feeds them; the lilies of the field do not spin or weave, and yet not even Solomon in all his glory was as magnificent as one of these.

Do not condemn: as you judge others, so will you yourself be judged. Before you criticize the speck of sawdust in another's eye, first remove the plank of wood in your own.

Ask, and it will be given to you; search, and you will find.

Avoid false prophets; beware of the wolf in sheep's clothing.

Anyone who hears my words and follows them is like the wise one who builds a house upon rock. When the rain comes, and the wind blows, and the floodwaters rise, the house will stand firm. But anyone who hears my words and ignores them is like the foolish one who builds a house upon sand. When the storm comes and the waters rise, the house will fall, because the foundations are built only on shifting sand.

MOUNT OF BEATITUDES
The Mount of Beatitudes is traditionally thought to be the place where Jesus gave his "sermon on the mount." The low hill is near Capernaum and overlooks the Sea of Galilee. The word "beatitude" means "blessed" and refers to the sayings of Jesus that begin "blessed are...." The beatitudes describe the qualities of the ideal follower of Jesus.

LILIES OF THE FIELD
When Jesus talked about the "lilies of the field" he may have been referring to anemones, shown above. In early spring these pretty flowers still cover the hills and fields of parts of the Middle East today.

The Sower

WHEREVER JESUS WENT, large numbers of men and women would follow. One day, Jesus was teaching by the Sea of Galilee. There were such crowds pressing around him that he got into a boat on the lake. All the people gathered by the water's edge to listen, and there he told them the parable of the sower.

There was a man sowing seed for the next year's harvest. As he walked along, scattering handfuls of wheat to the right and to the left, some of the seed fell on the beaten path, and this was quickly swooped on and eaten by birds. This is like the person who hears the word of God, but ignores its message. Satan, the evil one, will make sure they forget what they have heard.

SOWER'S BAG
A sower often carried his seed in a bag, like the one above. He sowed the seed by "broadcasting": he walked up and down the field and scattered seed along the way. Some seed was always lost, as in Jesus' parable.

As a man sows the seed, some falls on the beaten path and is eaten by birds

Some seed falls on shallow soil, so the wheat grows too quickly and is scorched by the sun

Some of the sower's seed fell where the soil lay very shallow, and because the earth was not deep enough for strong roots to take hold, the wheat grew too quickly. It was then scorched by the sun and withered and died. This is like the person who accepts the word of God, but who gives it little thought. When they are faced with any difficulty, their courage soon fails them, and they lose their faith.

Some seed fell among thistles, which grew tall and choked it. This is like the person who is lured by worldly pleasures, and whose heart is choked by ambition and a desire for wealth.

But some of the seed fell on good, fertile ground, and this seed ripened into a rich harvest. This is like the person who listens to the word of God, and loves and obeys the Lord. They will do much good in the world, and their efforts will be well rewarded.

SIFTING THE GRAIN
After harvesting, a woman would sift the grain. She held a sieve at an angle and shook it, while blowing across it to remove any husks. Stones collected at one end, and any broken pieces of grain fell through, leaving only the good grain.

The sower scatters handfuls of seed to the right and to the left

Some seed falls among thistles, which choke the wheat

Some seed falls on fertile ground and ripens into a rich harvest

The Death of John the Baptist

King Herod Antipas has John the Baptist thrown into prison

GREEK DANCING
In Jesus' time, Palestine was influenced by Greek, as well as Roman, culture. The Greeks often hired women dancers to entertain at banquets and festivals. This detail from a Greek bowl shows a woman dancing while drumming her tambourine. When Herodias' daughter, Salome, danced before Herod Antipas, she probably would have danced in a similar way.

KING HEROD ANTIPAS had John the Baptist thrown into prison, because the prophet dared condemn him for having married his brother's wife, Herodias. Herod both feared and admired John, but Herodias hated him. She wanted to see him put to death. Her husband, however, knew that John was a good man, and often listened to the Baptist's words of wisdom. Herod did not wish John dead, and so kept him well guarded in jail.

On Herod's birthday, he gave a supper to which he invited his lords and captains and all the big landowners of Galilee.

Herodias's daughter, Salome, a young girl of great beauty, danced before the king and his guests. Herod was so enchanted by her

On Herod's birthday, Salome dances before the king, and he promises that she can have anything she wishes

Herodias

King Herod

Salome

performance that he said to her, "Ask me for anything you please – half my kingdom if you wish – and it shall be yours."

The girl went over to her mother. "What shall I ask for?" she whispered.

Now Herodias had never forgiven the prophet for his condemnation of her marriage, and realized that now she could have her revenge. "Ask that the Baptist's head be brought to you on a dish," she said to her daughter.

When Herod heard Salome's request, he was appalled, but his promise had been made in front of the entire company, and he had no choice but to keep his word.

The order was quickly given, and John the Baptist executed in his prison cell. Soon afterward the prophet's bleeding head was carried into the banqueting hall on a silver platter, and placed at Salome's

BUT WHEN HEROD'S BIRTHDAY WAS KEPT, THE DAUGHTER OF HERODIAS DANCED BEFORE THEM, AND PLEASED HEROD. WHEREUPON HE PROMISED WITH AN OATH TO GIVE HER WHATSOEVER SHE WOULD ASK.

MATTHEW 14:6-7

Herodias tells Salome to ask for the head of John the Baptist

Herodias

John the Baptist's head is carried in on a silver platter

Salome

feet. Silently she picked it up and carried it to her mother.

John's followers, meanwhile, took the headless body and buried it. Then they went to Jesus to tell him what had happened. Jesus was deeply saddened by the news of the Baptist's death. In order to mourn for his friend, he left the crowds for a little while, going by boat to a place where he could be by himself to think and to pray.

The Good Samaritan

LAWLESS ROAD
Lone travelers on the road from Jerusalem to Jericho were easy prey for bandits. The quiet road drops steeply as it winds its way through rocky, desert land. It was ideal territory for robbers to hide in.

wine

olive oil

FIRST AID
The Samaritan put wine and oil on the wounds of the injured man. He would have applied wine first as an antiseptic. Then he would have soothed the wound by coating it with olive oil, before wrapping the cut in a linen bandage.

The thieves run away after attacking and robbing a man

A priest passes by the wounded man

A Levite passes by the wounded man

A Samaritan comes by and tends the man's wounds

NE DAY A LAWYER ASKED A QUESTION OF JESUS, thinking that he would trip him up. "What should I do," he asked, "to gain eternal life?"

"You know the law. What does that tell you?"

"You must love God with all your heart, and you must love your neighbor as you love yourself," said the lawyer.

"You have answered truly," Jesus said.

"But who is my neighbor?"

In reply, Jesus told the following story:

A man was traveling from Jerusalem to Jericho. On the way he was attacked by thieves, who stripped off his clothes, kicked and beat him, then left him half dead by the roadside. Not long afterward, a priest came by, and seeing the wounded man, crossed over to the other side. Next came a Levite, one of the men who assisted the priests in the temple. He, too, gave a quick look and then passed by on the far side of the road.

The third traveler to approach was a Samaritan. Seeing the man half conscious and covered in blood, he was filled with pity. Gently, he cleaned his wounds with wine and oil, before bandaging them with strips of linen. Then he put the stranger on his own donkey and took him to the nearest inn, where he looked after him all night. The following day before leaving, he gave the innkeeper money so that the invalid would have whatever he needed. "If you spend more than this, I will give you what is owed the next time I pass," he said.

"Now, which of these three men was the true neighbor?" Jesus asked the lawyer.

"The Samaritan."

"Just so. Remember this story, and behave to other people just as the good Samaritan did."

SAMARITAN
The picture above shows a Samaritan priest. Samaritans accept only the first five books of the Bible, the Torah, as the word of God. In Jesus' time the Samaritans lived in Samaria, in central Palestine. Many were descended from people who had settled in Israel after it was conquered by the Assyrians in 722 BC. The Samaritans and the Jews were sworn enemies. By using a Samaritan in his story, Jesus taught that one should be compassionate to everyone, to enemies as well as friends.

Samaritan

innkeeper

The Samaritan gives the innkeeper money and asks him to care for the wounded man

Lost and Found

A shepherd loses one of his hundred sheep

A LARGE CROWD HAD SURROUNDED Jesus to hear him speak. Among them were the Pharisees, who strictly observed and upheld the Jewish law. The Pharisees were horrified to see tax collectors and people who were law-breakers gathered around Jesus. They muttered to each other against him. "This man even eats with these sinners," they said.

But Jesus welcomed everyone, explaining that he had come to care for outcasts and all these who needed him.

Then he told a story, which compared God to a shepherd.

"God," he said, "is like a good shepherd with a flock of a hundred sheep. If he sees that one sheep is lost, that shepherd will leave the ninety-nine others and search the mountainside for his lost sheep. When he finds it, he will return home full of joy. He will rejoice more over the return of the one that had strayed than over all the rest of the flock that remained safe in the fold.

"For it is the will of God that no one, however humble, shall be lost."

THE GOOD SHEPHERD
God's care of the Israelites is often compared to that of a shepherd tending his sheep. In the New Testament, Jesus calls himself the Good Shepherd who cares, and finally dies, for his sheep.

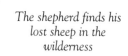

The shepherd finds his lost sheep in the wilderness

A woman sweeps the house searching for her lost coin

BROOM
The earth floors of houses had to be swept regularly to keep them free from dust and dirt. For this a woman would use a simple straw broom, such as the one above. The short handle meant that she had to stoop down.

Jesus then told the people another story about how much each person matters to God.

"Again, think of the woman who has ten pieces of silver: if she discovers one is missing, she lights her candle and searches the house until she finds it. And when she has found it, she will call her friends and neighbors together so they may rejoice with her. 'Look,' she said to them. 'How happy I am to have found the coin that was lost!'

"Just so, there is great joy among the angels in heaven when even one person turns away from wrong-doing."

After finding the coin, the woman calls on her friends to rejoice with her

The Prodigal Son

After leaving home, the farmer's younger son is reduced to looking after pigs

PODS
The pigs would have eaten pods from the carob, or locust tree. The pods are filled with a dark, sweet syrup.

PIGS
Middle Eastern, domestic pigs originated from the wild boar, shown above. To Jewish people, pigs symbolize greed and filth and are "unclean."

THE THIRD STORY JESUS TOLD was of the prodigal son. A rich farmer had two sons, and the youngest said to him one day, "Father, will you give me now my share of the property that is due to me?" His father agreed, and the young man took his share of money and goods, and left home to settle in a far country. There he lived like a prince, gambling and spending his money on rich clothes and jewels. Night after night he entertained crowds of friends with dancing girls and the most expensive wines.

In time, he spent all his money, and as he grew poor, the country fell into famine. The young man's friends disappeared, his possessions were sold to pay his debts, and when he begged in the street for food, everyone he approached turned away. Eventually, he was hired by a farmer, who sent him into the fields to watch over the pigs. He was so hungry that he longed to eat the pods that he fed to the pigs.

In despair he said to himself, "My father has

The youngest son returns home to his father, who embraces him joyfully

many servants, all of them well clothed and fed, and here am I, his son, penniless and starving! I will go to him now and beg his forgiveness and see if I may work for him as a servant."

His father saw him coming from a long way off. Overjoyed, he ran to meet his son, threw his arms about his neck, and kissed him.

"Father, I have done wrong to God and to you. I am not worthy to be called your son." But immediately, his father gestured to him to be silent and called for his best robe to be brought out. "Put a ring on his hand, and soft shoes on his feet," he commanded. "And kill the fattest calf, for tonight we shall have a feast. My son, whom I believed to be dead, has come home!"

When the elder brother returned that evening from working in the fields, he was astonished to hear the sound of music and dancing. "What is the meaning of this?" he asked one of his men.

"Your brother has come home, and your father is holding a feast in his honor."

The elder brother was furious, and refused to enter the house. Soon his father came out to see what was wrong. "Father, how could you treat me like this? I, who have worked hard all these years, have never received anything from you. And yet for your other son, who left home and squandered his inheritance, you kill the fattest calf!"

"My son, you are very dear to me, and everything I have belongs to you. But your brother was lost, and now he is found, and it is right that we celebrate his return!"

So it is that God will forgive all who, having abandoned him, return. And, like the father in the parable, he will rejoice at their coming back.

HARVEST

The farmer's elder son may have been helping his father with the harvest when the prodigal, or wasteful, son returned. Harvesting was a busy time and the farmer's whole family helped to gather the crops. The workers used a sickle to cut the grain. They held the stalks in one hand and cut them close to the ears of wheat with the sickle. It had a short handle and a rounded iron blade, like the one above. The cut stalks were laid on the ground, and the workers tied the stalks together into sheaves. The stalks were then taken away in carts for threshing.

"WE SHOULD MAKE MERRY, AND BE GLAD: FOR THIS THY BROTHER WAS DEAD, AND IS ALIVE AGAIN; AND WAS LOST, AND IS FOUND."
LUKE 15:31-32

A feast is held to celebrate the son's return

The elder son is angry: he has worked for his father for years, and has never received anything

His father tells his son that everything he has belongs to him

The Unmerciful Servant

The servant falls on his knees in front of the king and begs for time to repay his debt

PETER CAME TO JESUS and asked him a question. "Lord, how many times should I forgive a man who has done me wrong? Up to seven times?"

"Not seven times, but seventy times seven: there should be no limit to forgiveness," said Jesus, and to show what he meant he told his disciples a story.

There was a king who was good to his servants, often lending them large sums of money.

The day came when the accounts had to be settled. There was one man who was brought before the king whose debt was so large that he had no hope of repaying it. "As you cannot pay," said the king, "I shall seize all your possessions and sell you and your wife and children into slavery."

The servant fell on his knees. "Sir, I beg you have pity on me! Give me time and I will raise the money and pay back everything!"

The king was moved by the man's despair, and raising him up told him that the whole of his huge debt was canceled, and that he was free to go.

Soon afterward this same man came across a fellow servant who owed him a small sum of money. He took him by the throat and demanded, "Pay me what you owe me now!" The fellow servant fell to his knees and begged the man for mercy.

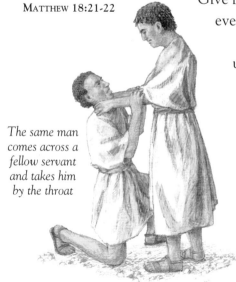

The same man comes across a fellow servant and takes him by the throat

He demands that he repay the small sum of money he owes him

"I cannot pay this debt just now! Please have pity! Give me time and I will raise the money, I promise!"

But the servant showed no pity, and had the man thrown into prison, until he could pay back the debt.

The other servants were shocked by what they saw, and went to tell their master what had happened.

The king instantly summoned the man to come before him. "When you begged for mercy, I showed you mercy, and yet you had none for a man who owed you far less than you owed me. Now you shall be punished!"

And the king gave orders for his heartless servant to be taken away to jail.

"Just so," said Jesus, "this is how your heavenly Lord will treat each of you unless you forgive those who have done you wrong from the bottom of your heart."

SERVANT
This Roman carving dates from around AD 200 and shows a servant grinding spices. In Jesus' time a servant was either a slave or a hired worker who was paid for his work and was free to leave when he wished.

The king gives orders for his heartless servant to be jailed

Lazarus and the Rich Man

A rich man feasts every day

Lazarus longs to eat the scraps from the rich man's table

Dogs lick Lazarus' sores

ABRAHAM SAID, "SON, REMEMBER THAT THOU IN THY LIFETIME RECEIVEDST THY GOOD THINGS, AND LIKEWISE LAZARUS EVIL THINGS: BUT NOW HE IS COMFORTED, AND THOU ART TORMENTED."

LUKE 16:25

ESUS TOLD A STORY to warn people about God's judgment of the selfish.

There was once a rich man who dressed in the finest silks and linens. Every day he feasted off the most delicious dishes and drank the best wine. But at his gate lay a poor beggar called Lazarus. His body was thin and frail. He was covered in sores that would not heal, and wild dogs came and licked them. He longed to eat the scraps that fell from the rich man's table.

The day came when Lazarus died and was carried by the angels to Heaven. The rich man died soon after, but he went to Hell where he suffered in torment. Looking upward, he saw Lazarus in Heaven, and he cried out to Abraham, father of his people, "Help me! I am being burnt alive! Send Lazarus to dip his finger in water, so that he may cool my tongue!"

"No, Lazarus shall not come to you," Abraham replied. "On Earth he had nothing, while you were surrounded by luxury. It is right that he should now enjoy happiness while you are left to suffer punishment."

"Will you allow him then to go and warn my five brothers what may lie in store for them? If they saw a messenger from the dead, they would believe him and repent."

"They have the words of the prophets to guide them," said Abraham. "If they do not listen to them, then neither will they listen if someone returns from the dead."

The Pharisee and the Tax Collector

JESUS TOLD THE FOLLOWING STORY to show how important it is not to be conceited or to look down on others:

Two men went to the temple to pray. One was a Pharisee, the other a collector of taxes. The Pharisee stood in the middle of the court, and addressed God confidently. "I thank you, Lord, that I am so much better than other men, that I am not dishonest nor corrupt, that I am superior in every way to people like that little tax collector over there!"

The tax collector stood meekly in a corner, believing himself unworthy even to raise his eyes toward Heaven. Bowing his head, he whispered, "Please, Lord, show mercy to me, a sinner."

"Now," said Jesus, "it was the tax collector who went home with his sins forgiven. Everyone who thinks themselves higher than others will be humbled; everyone who is humble will be lifted high."

prayer shawl

phylactery

AT PRAYER
Jewish men wore prayer shawls and phylacteries during times of prayer. The shawl had a striped border. Phylacteries were small boxes made of black leather that held tiny strips of parchment. Four passages from the Torah, the first five books of the Bible, were written on the strips. One box was worn strapped to the forehead, and another was tied to the upper left arm, near the heart. This was a sign that God's teachings were controlling the person's thoughts and feelings and that both the head and the heart are used when seeing God. Many Jews still wear prayer shawls and phylacteries today.

The tax collector prays in the corner

The Pharisee prays in the middle of the court

"EVERY ONE THAT EXALTETH HIMSELF SHALL BE ABASED; AND HE THAT HUMBLETH HIMSELF SHALL BE EXALTED."
LUKE 18:14

Jesus and the Children

THE TWELVE DISCIPLES WERE ARGUING among themselves about who would be considered the most worthy in the eyes of God. Jesus, overhearing their discussion, called them to him and questioned them. But the disciples remained silent, because they were ashamed of what they had been saying. Jesus said to them, "In God's kingdom, he who wishes to be first, must be last: he who wishes to come first before God must live humbly while on Earth, and put others before himself."

A group of children came running up to Jesus and clustered around him. The disciples started to push them away, but Jesus was annoyed and stopped them. "These are my children," he told the disciples. "All children must be free to come to me when they wish, for the kingdom of Heaven belongs to all who are as innocent as they."

Then he picked up one child and set her on his knee. "Look at this little one," he said. "Unless you are as open and trusting as this child, you will have no chance of entering Heaven." Then he stretched out his hands and blessed the children.

glass marbles

stone marbles

CHILDREN'S GAMES
Marbles were very popular with children in Jesus' time. Children also played with whistles, rattles, hoops, and spinning tops. Jesus said that to enter God's kingdom, people must be like children, innocent and trusting.

Children come to be near Jesus

Jesus says to his disciples they must be like children if they are to enter Heaven

The Rich Young Man

YOUNG MAN from a rich family came running up to Jesus and knelt before him. "Lord, what must I do to gain eternal life?"

"Have you kept all the commandments?" Jesus asked him.

"I have, Lord."

"Then nothing remains but for you to sell everything you own, distribute your money among the poor, and follow me. Then you will find your treasure in Heaven."

The young man looked appalled, for he had great possessions, and sadly he turned away. Jesus looked at him with love, understanding how difficult it was for such a man to give up all that he owned. "You see," he said to the disciples, "it is easier for a camel to go through the eye of a needle than for a rich man to enter the kingdom of God."

"But what about us?" asked Peter. "We have left everything behind, our homes, our families, to follow you."

"Anyone who has done what you have done will be rewarded many times over on Earth and in Heaven," Jesus reassured him.

JESUS ANSWERETH AGAIN, AND SAITH UNTO THEM, "CHILDREN, HOW HARD IS IT FOR THEM THAT TRUST IN RICHES TO ENTER INTO THE KINGDOM OF GOD! IT IS EASIER FOR A CAMEL TO GO THROUGH THE EYE OF A NEEDLE, THAN FOR A RICH MAN TO ENTER INTO THE KINGDOM OF GOD."
MARK 10:24-25

On hearing he must give up everything he owns, the young man walks sadly away

A rich young man kneels before Jesus and asks what he should do to gain eternal life

Zacchaeus the Tax Collector

*The crowds gather around Jesus, but Zacchaeus is too
small to see over the people in front of him*

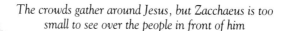

Zacchaeus

"ZACCHAEUS, MAKE
HASTE, AND COME
DOWN; FOR TODAY I
MUST ABIDE AT THY
HOUSE."
LUKE 19:5

*Zacchaeus climbs
a sycamore tree
to see Jesus*

SYCAMORE TREE
The sycamore tree was
often planted along
roadways in Palestine to
provide shade for travelers.
Zacchaeus would have
found it easy to climb its
low-lying branches.

*Jesus calls to Zacchaeus to come
down from the tree*

ESUS HAD ARRIVED in Jericho. Pushing through the crowd was a rich man, a chief tax collector called Zacchaeus. He was eager to set eyes on Jesus, but because he was small, he could neither force his way through the crowd, nor see over the people in front of him. Finally, in desperation, he ran ahead, and climbed up into a sycamore tree that stood beside the road he knew Jesus would take.

As Jesus passed beneath the tree, he looked up and saw Zacchaeus sitting astride one of its branches. "Zacchaeus, come down from there! Take me to your house – I'd like to stay with you for a while."

Zacchaeus was overjoyed, and ran home as fast as he could to prepare a welcome. But others began to murmur resentfully. "How shocking," they said, "that he should stay with such a sinner!"

But when Jesus arrived at the house Zacchaeus said to him, "I will give to the poor half of everything I own. And if I have cheated anyone, I will repay that man with four times the amount I took from him dishonestly."

Jesus said, "Today a man has been saved!" And he blessed Zacchaeus, and went full of joy into his house.

TAX COLLECTOR
In Jesus' time, tax collecting, banking, and money-changing were practiced in the open air, as in this stone carving from the 3rd century AD. Tax collectors set up simple wooden tables and people came to them to pay their taxes. People disliked tax collectors because they worked for the conquering Romans, and because they often swindled people. By being friendly with a tax collector, Jesus showed that his message was for all people.

Zacchaeus welcomes Jesus into his home and says that he will give half of everything he owns to the poor

Zacchaeus

Jesus

Workers in the Vineyard

*A group of laborers is hired
to work in a vineyard*

*Throughout the day, more
laborers are hired*

*The laborers who were hired
first grumble because they
have been paid the same as
those who came later*

vineyard owner

VINEYARD
These women are sorting
and packing grapes in a
vineyard near Bethlehem.
Vineyards were common
throughout Palestine in
Jesus' time. The vines
were planted in rows and
the branches were trained
along sticks. Each
vineyard had a
watchtower, from which a
worker could keep a look-
out for thieves, animals,
and birds. Wealthy
farmers hired workers to
help with the harvest.

J ESUS ONCE TOLD A PARABLE about a man who
owned a big vineyard. One morning he went to the
marketplace and hired some laborers, offering to pay each
man one denarius for a day's work. A little later the same man saw
a group standing by idly with nothing to do. "Go and work in my
vineyard," he said. Delighted, the men accepted his offer.

Three more times the man hired more workers, until the sun was
low in the sky and the day nearly over.

That evening the man told his steward to summon the laborers and
pay them their wages. "Pay first those who started work last," he told
him, "and give one denarius to each man."

However, when the men who had been toiling in the heat since
early morning saw that they were to get no more than those who had
started work at the very end of the day, they began to grumble. "We
have worked longer hours, so we deserve more pay," they complained.

"No," said the man. "I offered to pay each of you one denarius, and
to this you agreed. You are all equal in my eyes."

So, in the kingdom of Heaven those who come late to God are
loved and valued as much as those who have always been with him.

The Wedding Feast

ONE EVENING, when dining at the house of a rich Pharisee, Jesus told this parable to explain the kingdom of Heaven:

There was a king who prepared a magnificent feast for his son's wedding. When everything was ready, he sent out his servants to summon the guests. But none of them would come. Again the servants went out to invite them, but each one had found an excuse for not attending.

One said, "I have just bought a new team of oxen and want to work on my farm."

Another said, "I want to inspect my new piece of land."

A third said, "I am newly married, I cannot come."

Angry, the king said, "Those who turned down my invitation were not worthy." He gave orders that all the beggars, the sick, and the blind should be asked in from the surrounding countryside. "They shall sit at my table and be entertained at my feast!" said the king.

Later that night, as the king wandered among his guests, he noticed one who was not dressed in wedding clothes. "Why do you come here to celebrate a wedding wearing such a garment?" he asked him. But the man remained speechless. "Throw him out into the darkness!" said the king.

"So it is," said Jesus, "that many are invited to God's kingdom, but only those who come in the right spirit will be allowed in."

One guest will not come to the wedding feast because he wants to work with his new team of oxen

Another guest wants to inspect his land

Another guest says he is newly married

Beggars, the sick, and the blind are then invited to the wedding feast

The king throws out one guest for not wearing wedding clothes

The Wise and Foolish Maidens

Ten maidens fall asleep while waiting for the bridegroom

Five wise maidens have extra oil for their lamps

jar of oil

Five foolish maidens have nothing

oil lamp

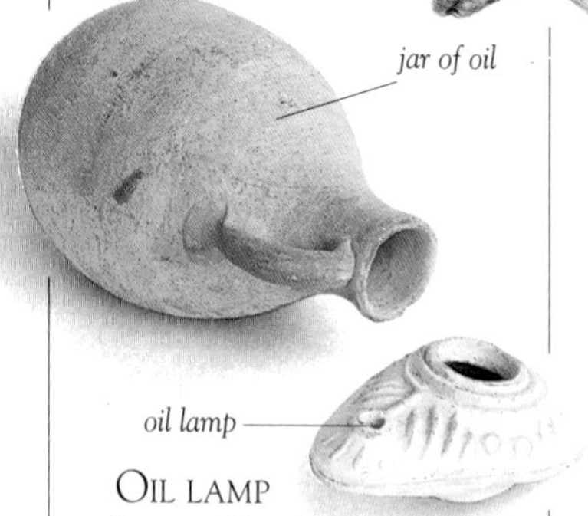

OIL LAMP
Lamps like the one above were common in Jesus' time. Oil was poured into the hole in the middle and a wick was placed in the end hole. The oil would last for about three hours, so it was important to have extra oil close by.

TO EXPLAIN THE KINGDOM OF HEAVEN, Jesus told the following story:

There were ten young women at a wedding feast who went one evening to wait for the bridegroom's procession to arrive, all of them carrying lamps. Now five of the women were wise, five were foolish. The wise ones carried jars of extra oil for their lamps; but the foolish ones took nothing.

The bridegroom was late in arriving, so one by one the young women fell asleep. Then at midnight, a cry was heard: "The bridegroom is coming! Quickly, go out to meet him!" The maidens arose, and went to trim their lamps before going out into the darkness. The five foolish young women found that their lamps had gone out from lack of oil. "Please," they asked the others, "give us some of your oil." "No," the wise maidens replied. "If we do that, there will not be enough to go around. You must buy some more oil for yourselves."

So the five foolish girls went to buy oil, and while they were gone the bridegroom arrived. The wise maidens welcomed him, and he took them with him into the wedding, shutting the door behind him.

When the foolish maidens returned, they beat with their fists on the closed door. "Sir, sir, please let us in!"

But the bridegroom answered, "I do not know you, therefore I cannot let you inside."

"So," said Jesus, "always be prepared, for you do not know when the son of God will come."

The five foolish maidens
go to buy oil

While they are gone, the bridegroom arrives and
takes the wise maidens to the wedding

The Parable of the Talents

first servant   second servant   third servant

A man gives a sum of
money to each of his
three servants

JESUS TOLD A PARABLE that
compared the kingdom of
Heaven to a man who, about to
set out on a long journey, entrusted his
servants with the care of his property. To
each of them he gave a sum of money.

To the first and most senior he gave five
talents; to the second servant, two talents;
and to the third, one talent; so that each
was paid according to his ability.

The first servant took his five talents
and cleverly bought and sold so that
before long he had doubled his money.
The second servant did the same,
returning with twice the sum he had been
given. The third servant, however, went
away and dug a hole in the ground and
buried his talent.

*To the first servant he gives five talents;
to the second, two talents; and to the
third, one talent*

BUT HE THAT HAD RECEIVED
ONE TALENT WENT AND
DIGGED IN THE EARTH, AND
HID HIS LORD'S MONEY.
MATTHEW 25:18

After a while their master returned and he asked them what they
had done with their money. He praised the first two for having made
the most of what they were given. "You are good and faithful

*The first servant buys and sells and
doubles his five talents*

*The second servant buys and sells
and doubles his two talents*

*The third servant digs a hole in the
ground and buries his one talent*

servants," he said, "You have been faithful with a few things – so I will put you in charge of many things."

But when the third servant came to him and returned his one talent, saying that he had simply hidden his coins in the ground, his master was very angry. "How stupid and ungrateful you are! At least you should have put the money in a bank where it would have earned interest." And he gave orders that the man should be thrown out of the house, and his one talent taken from him and given to the servant who now had ten.

So it is that we must make the most of what God gives us, and then we will be prepared to enter the kingdom of Heaven.

MONEY
The silver coins above are Roman denarii, which were commonly used in Jesus' time. Worth about a day's wage, each denarius had the head of the Roman emperor engraved on one side. A talent was not a coin, but a unit of weight equal to about 66 pounds (30 kg). In the parable it represents a large amount of money, the equivalent of several years' wages.

The first two servants are praised for making the most of what they were given

The third servant returns his one talent to his master

The man is angry with the third servant for not doing anything with his money

Jesus Enters Jerusalem

Two of Jesus' disciples find a donkey with its colt, and return with the little donkey

ESUS AND HIS DISCIPLES were on their way to Jerusalem. When they reached Bethphage on the Mount of Olives, which was only a short distance from the city, Jesus sent two of his followers into the village. "You will find a donkey with its colt tethered to a doorway," he said. "Untie the young donkey and bring it here. If anyone tries to stop you, say, 'The Lord has need of it,' and they will let you go in peace."

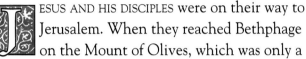

Jesus rides toward Jerusalem on a donkey's colt

DONKEY AND COLT
In biblical times, royalty would ride on a donkey during periods of peace, rather than a horse, which was associated with war. When Jesus rode into Jerusalem on a colt, or young donkey, he fulfilled a prophecy that a king would come in peace and humility to Jerusalem.

Crowds gather around Jesus, singing and shouting his praises to the sky

Palm leaves are laid in Jesus' path

The disciples did as Jesus had told them. Returning with the little colt, they put their cloaks on its back to act as a saddle. It had never been ridden before, but with Jesus it was docile and obedient. And so the Son of God rode into Jerusalem on a donkey.

When the people saw him coming, they covered the road with their garments and cut palm leaves and laid them in his path. Crowds gathered before him and behind him, singing, and shouting his praises to the sky. "Blessed is he, the son of David! Blessed is he who is coming in the name of the Lord! Peace in Heaven and glory in the highest!"

As Jesus drew nearer to Jerusalem he wept, for he knew that soon

PALM LEAVES
The people laid palm leaves in Jesus' path. These long, feathery leaves, which look like branches, grow from the top of the tall, slender trunk of the date palm. Palm leaves were a symbol of grace and of victory.

"BLESSED IS HE THAT COMETH IN THE NAME OF THE LORD; HOSANNA IN THE HIGHEST."
MATTHEW 21:9

Jesus and his followers pass through a gate into Jerusalem

THE HOLY CITY
Jerusalem is the Holy City to Jews, Christians, and Muslims, and pilgrims flock to the city every year. In the picture above, a Greek Orthodox priest walks along the Via Dolorosa in the Old City of Jerusalem where Jesus is believed to have carried the cross.

great troubles would come to Jerusalem.

Jesus and his followers passed through the gate into the city and made their way toward the temple. The people of Jerusalem stared to see such a procession. "Who is this man?" they asked. "Why is he being honored in this way?"

"That is Jesus," the others replied. "He is the great prophet from Nazareth in Galilee."

Jesus and the Temple Traders

WESTERN WALL
In front of the Dome of the Rock, a Muslim mosque, stands the Western Wall, the only remaining part of Herod's temple.

"MY HOUSE SHALL BE CALLED
THE HOUSE OF PRAYER; BUT
YE HAVE MADE IT A DEN
OF THIEVES."
MATTHEW 21:13

JESUS WENT TO THE TEMPLE in Jerusalem. Its courtyards were a marketplace, with people buying and selling, changing money and haggling over the price of cattle. In a fury Jesus threw over the tables of the money changers so that the coins poured on the ground, and drove out the traders with their oxen and sheep. "The house of God is a house of prayer," he thundered, "but you have turned it into a den of thieves!"

Once the temple had been cleared, people came to Jesus to be healed. But when some of the chief priests and the teachers of the law saw the eager crowds surrounding him, and when they heard the children singing, "Hosanna to the son of David!" they were uneasy. "Do you know what these children are saying?" they asked him.

"Yes," Jesus replied. "Have you never read the Scriptures that say that it is innocent children who praise God most sweetly?"

Then Jesus left for Bethany, where he stayed the

The traders gather in the temple courtyard

night, returning the next day with his disciples to begin teaching in the temple. Many chief priests and teachers of law were waiting for him. "Who gave you permission to teach here?" they demanded.

Jesus replied, "I will ask you one question, and if you can answer it, then I will tell you by whose authority I am here. The question is this: was it God or was it men who gave John the right to baptize?"

The priests were puzzled. "If we say God gave to him that right, he will ask, then why did you not believe him? And if we say, it was men, then the people will turn against us and stone us, for they look on John as a prophet."

So they said to Jesus, "We cannot tell." And Jesus said, "Then neither can I tell you by whose authority I am here."

SCALES
In Jesus' time money changers and traders used scales similar to these Roman bronze scales for weighing money and produce. The money changers changed people's foreign currency into shekels for use in the temple. They often made an unfair profit, and it was this that Jesus objected to when he drove them out of the temple.

Jesus drives the traders out of the temple

The chief priests and the teachers of the law are angered by Jesus

Index

Who's Who in the Bible Stories

ANDREW The fisherman brother of Simon Peter. One of the 12 disciples. *Pages 30-31*

ANNA An elderly woman who saw Jesus when he was presented in the Temple. *Page 19*

AUGUSTUS The Roman emperor during the time of Jesus. *Page 14*

BARTHOLOMEW One of the 12 disciples. *Page 31*

ELIZABETH The cousin of Mary and the mother of John the Baptist. *Pages 9, 12, 13*

GABRIEL The angel who announced to Mary that she would give birth to Jesus. *Pages 9-11*

HEROD THE GREAT Ruler of Judea when Jesus was born. Pages 20, 22

HEROD ANTIPAS Son of Herod the great. Ordered John the Baptist's execution. *Pages 36-37*

HEROD ARCHELAUS Son of Herod the Great, and a ruler of Judea. *Page 22*

JAMES The name of two of the 12 disciples. *Pages 30-31*

JESUS CHRIST Regarded by Christians as the Son of God, and the Messiah predicted in the Old Testament. The main focus of Christian faith and the central figure in the New Testament. *Pages 14-61*

JOHN One of the 12 disciples, the brother of James. He wrote the fourth Gospel. *Pages 6, 30-31*

JOHN THE BAPTIST Jesus' cousin who prepared people for his coming. *Pages 8-11, 26-27, 36-37*

JOSEPH The husband of Mary. *Pages 10, 14-19, 22, 24-25*

JUDAS ISCARIOT The disciple who betrayed Jesus. *Page 31*

LAZARUS The poor man in Jesus' parable. *Pages 46-47*

LUKE A doctor who wrote one of the Gospels. *Page 6*

MARK The writer of one of the four Gospels. His mother's house in Jerusalem was a meeting place for the early Church. *Page 6*

MARY The mother of Jesus. *Pages 10-12, 14-19, 21, 22, 24-25*

MATTHEW A tax collector who became one of the 12 disciples. The writer of one of the Gospels. *Pages 6, 30-31*

PETER A fisherman who became one of the 12 disciples and a close friend of Jesus. *Pages 31, 44*

PHILIP One of the 12 disciples *Page 31*

PONTIUS PILATE The Roman governor who ordered the crucifixion of Jesus. Map on title page

SALOME The daughter of Herodias who danced in front of King Herod and asked for the head of John the Baptist. (Not referred to by name in the Bible). *Pages 36-37*

SATAN The name sometimes given to the Devil, who is thought to be the source of all sin and evil. *Pages 28-29, 34*

SIMEON The elderly man who saw Jesus presented in the Temple. *Pages 18-19*

SIMON One of the 12 disciples. *Page 31*

THADDAEUS One of the 12 disciples. *Page 31*

THOMAS One of the 12 disciples. He doubted at first that Jesus had risen from the dead. *Page 31*

ZACCHAEUS The tax collector who climbed a tree to see Jesus. *Pages 50-51*

ZECHARIAH The father of John the Baptist. *Pages 8-11*

Acknowledgments

Photographic Credits
l=left, r=right, t=top, c=center
b=bottom

ASAP:/Lev Borodulin 33br.
Bridgeman Art Library: 6c, 6cr, 6bl, 6br
British. Library; 7t Agnew & Sons; 11tr
British Library.
Bruce Coleman LTD: 27br.
DAS/Jamie Simpson 59br.
Sonia Halliday: 10tl, 28tl 52cl, 58bl, 60bl

Robert Harding Picture Library: 15tr, 24tl, 33tr.
Image Bank: 13tr.
Erich Lessing Archive: 8tl, 40bl, 45tr.
NHPA:/Vincente Garcia Canseco 42bl.
Dino Politis: 30bl
Zev Radovan: 9tr, 12bl, 19tr, 27tr, 29tr, 38tl, 50bl.
Rheinisches Landesmuseum, Trier: 51tr.
Scala: 21tr, 36bl.
Harry Smith Collection: 42cl.

DK would like to thank:
Tim Ridley, Nick Goodall and Gary Ombler at the DK Studio; Dorian Spencer Davies; Antonio Forcione; Christopher Gillingwater; Polly Goodman; George Hart; Alan Hills; James W. Hunter; Robin Hunter; Marcus James; Anna Kunst; Michelle de Larrabeiti; Antonio Montoro; Anderley Moore; Jackie Ogburn; Derek Peach; Lenore Person; Dino Politis; Lara Tankel Holtz and Martin Wilson for their help in producing this book.

Picture research by: Diana Morris

Index by: Lynn Bresler